SHADES OF GREEN

Kathy
Thank you supporting
and connecting!
keep building!
— Glenance

glenancegreen@gmail.
com

SHADES OF GREEN

Written By

GLENANCE GREEN

Illustrated By
Ayza-Andriana Churina

ISBN: 0692793453
ISBN 13: 9780692793459

I rarely revisit the things I have written and performed years ago. One day while in search of another book, I came across an old journal filled with thoughts and poetry. Anxiously flipping through the pages as if it were a new read, I realized that some of what I wrote back then resonated with me in that moment. I thought to myself, I could have easily written this yesterday or last week or six months ago. It all felt so...relevant. That was the birth of this anthology. My editor was concerned about my use of this term. She reminded me that an anthology is a collection of literary works chosen by the compiler. She was concerned about the reader believing that there are multiple authors writing the selections included and therefore suggested that I use the term *collection*. But I didn't, and I'm not going to because I'm all about breaking the rules of a genre when my work is relevant but does not fit into the neat little box prepackaged by contributors before me. I am the compiler and this is my collection of literary works. To be clear, it is anthological in the sense that it is a series or collection of thoughts, poetry, prose, and short stories developed over time, each distinct from one another yet perfectly intertwined in the art form that I have chosen, just as it has chosen me. Much of what is included was written for the purpose of this text, though a great deal is from the past finding its way to me in the present, hence the title *Shades of Green*. It serves as a reminder of where I have been and an indicator of where I am going. The evolution of myself in woman form designed black breathes life onto every page.

I have spent a lot of time in heavy reflection. While in reflection I have discovered and rediscovered myself over and over again, counting every experience both good and bad as a lesson learned. In those deep dark periods, I found love. Not the *one size fits all* standard of love that we use ever so loosely in our everyday language, but love in many forms —those that can be defined but not described in merely one word in the English language. Understanding love in its complex and multidimensional forms, I began to express *love* more freely. Love became more than a feeling. It was a verb manifesting itself as a way of life in every domain of my existence that I deemed important. To illustrate *love* according to how I see it in my mind and experience it in real life, I deconstructed seven forms of Greek love. Love, as described in the Greek language, provides the nuanced understandings most closely aligned to my non-linear trail of thoughts. I use the imagery of Greek love —as manifested in my mind and brought to life by my artist (Shout out to Ayza-Andriana Churina!) —to shape a narrative, one in which is considerate of context, culture, politics, structures, and constructs as determinates of our realities.

Since there is something to be gained for everyone, this read is intended for all audiences. However, I dedicate this book to my courageous mother, LaVerne Denise Green (Hayes); my steadfast cousin, Abigail Hayes; and all of the melanin queens still in search of their magic. You are powerful beyond measure! May a word propel inspiration, healing, joy, and reflection. May a phrase intertwine our hearts and minds in solidarity and support of one another. And may a stanza provide affirmations and assurance that you are not alone.

This Piece

I discovered love in many forms.

Each distinctly beautiful from the last.

Different forms of love not yet captured by the English language.

Each bearing a different burden of pleasure and pain.

Residing in words. Verses. Phrases. Visual images indescribable to the human tongue, only in spiritual haikus.

Moments of expression built from my reality.

From beautiful people and seemingly opulent things to the hyperconstructions of a social reality not yet realized, predetermined to be unimaginable.

A mere perspective for others.

The vulnerable essences of everyday life for me.

The birth of this piece?

At the place where family, friends, partners, lovers, myself, and God as the essence of the universe converge.

This piece?

Is not for your comfort, though it may soothe your soul.

This piece?

Is not for your displeasure, though you might disagree.

This piece?

Is simply this piece.

Only *the woke* will reflect.

Come away with me!

—G

When I dare to be powerful, to use my strength in the service of my vision, then it becomes less and less important whether I am afraid.

—Audre Lorde

While the poetry of social movements is rarely seriously considered in debates about alternatives to neoliberalism, its significance for understanding the present moment cannot be overstated.

—Jordan T. Camp, *Incarcerating the Crisis: Freedom Struggles and the Rise of the Neoliberal State*, 2016

Contents

PHILAUTIA

Self-love and Resilience

Wherefore Art Thou, Woman Who Is Black?

I love myself.

The pigmentation of melanin in my skin that the sun favors and the moon protects.

The curvature of my nose and outline of my lips.

The small of my back and my ancestors' hips.

Descendant of slaves in a land not yet free.

For this treatment of my people is what has made me, *me*.

I love myself.

And not in that self-absorbed, egoistic, pompous, high sadity manner; though I do recognize that my beauty is unparalleled.

Not beauty as many may comprehend, in their ethnocentric colonial understanding of the term.

But the visages of the motherland made colloquial.

I love myself.

The quirky way that I think, the embarrassing way that I speak, and spontaneity in the way that I move.

I love how I understand my flaws, especially when we cross paths and I can see bits and pieces of my reflection in you.

Every flaw is God's perfection.

And since I am a perfectionist, my flaws give me cause to seek improvement to be the best version of myself that I can be because...

I love me.

For being different. For not conforming to your standard of blackness...or womanhood...or black womanhood while you ascribe and reify my masculine attributes and exclude me from the category of gender because my femininity is unfamiliar to you.

I love me.

For being different. And articulately vocal and proud of my difference, despite your levels of comfort and soft perpetuation of lies that we only look different but are one and the same.

"We all bleed red."

No. I bleed pain. I bleed suffering. I bleed hope. I bleed fragility. I bleed love. Lifting black men up on my shoulders even when they do not see me or understand that they need a boost to level up to life. Carrying black women on my back just to encourage them to keep moving because life has thrown them a number, and it has never been *one*.

I love myself.

And not because I'm a member of the *human* race but a race that has travailed and overcome amidst great odds. For the yoke has never been easy and the burden has never been light.

I love myself.

Slangified broken English and code switching included.

Gyrating to good music on Friday nights. Monday morning, suited and booted.

I love myself.

Oh, woman! Mother of creation! Wherefore art thou?

You can shake her violently, but her magic dust will never fall.

Oh, woman, who embodies the queerness of a past that haunts her because she hasn't quite discovered how to live free. Wherefore art thou?

Her resiliency is not a euphemism for tokenism.

I love myself.

Phenomenally.

This Melanin Moment

Shoot me dead in the streets
And watch me fold into the concrete
Let my lifeless body be a testament to just how powerful I am—
ahem—we are

Talk down to me when my English doesn't match your vernacular
Critique me when my uncombed hair isn't to your standard of
presentable
Fire me when my natural curves fill out these knee-length skirts
and ankle-rubbing dresses
Tell me that I'm not a good *fit* for what you're looking for, yet steal
my swag for your campaign of non-melanated bodies swangin'
slang and Columbusing for profit
Always *discovering* something that has already been found

No, these dreadlocks do not belong to you. For if they did, they
would not appear dreadful while our texture of hair supports a
beautiful loc
No shade to the surgeons, but can black women get a share of your
profits?
Papier mâché'ing our lips and thighs and butt and hips
Patenting the black women's body, reprinting and distributing her
beauty to all while simultaneously demeaning and denigrating her
in the process; holding her in contempt for the way God made her
in *Her* image

Tell us that we're socially undesirable
For if we discovered just how desirable we really were, the world—
including our own—would request the original on demand, and
not the replicates

Ode to this Melanin moment
Where my people are continuously executed because of the color
of our skin
The darker the pigment, the higher the threat, the sweeter the
death to the hearts of the hatred
Where blackness exists beyond a law of protection
Where intersecting identities become distinct assemblages of
personhood, unrelated yet related, while seemingly functioning
with uniformity as one

Ode to this Melanin moment
Where everything is taken away and what's left is our bare, flawless
skin
Where difference doesn't matter, until it does
Ah, yet difference is a beautiful thing

Ode to this Melanin moment
Where my pride cannot be forsaken
Where I'm unapologetically black and can still find love to give
despite what has been taken
Where transgressions are forgiven
Oh, how the universe can be so kind
Where dry tears are wiped, even though we know you'll be just fine

Ode to this Melanin moment
Blessings blazing upon my trail
With each door I kick down, I know I'm living
Even when I'm dying a slow death, I'm still reaching beyond the ceiling

Ode to this Melanin moment
Where Melanin remains the one thing that cannot be taken away
Where black and brown meets sexy with no option for whether they'll stay
Where everything and nothing is taken for granted, even in moments of solace and despair
Where virtue is black and love is blacker, empirically testing our bodies for hope and care

Ode to this Melanin moment
Where I'm 29 but look as if I'm a pubescent youth
Where my mother is 57 but looks like she's 32
Oh, how wicked powerful is this magical fountain of youth

Ode to this Melanin moment
Oh, how fantastical we are
Existing in a space yet not existent for this beautiful Melanin moment

Victory

Watching the sun as it sets over the horizon where the sky meets the concrete.

It looks half empty but the ground looks half full swallowing a light full of energy.

Bodies moving swiftly as darkness leave their shadows and covers the pavement for miles on end.

And when the sun goes down, I look out of my window and stare into the night, my glass of hope, that by daybreak I would be more accomplished. Stable. Less restless.

My diaphragm is wheezing, cold and out of the breath that I have been using to breathe life into my reality.

Constantly feeling as if I'm not good enough, always looking for more. I'm stagnant.

Feeling my heart beat for love, my cries to the earth seem to be in vain.

But *She* gives me blood in exchange for my tears in hopes that I can save a life with words that can connect to a heart so heavy and weak that it is unsure if it will make it to tomorrow because yesterday was never supposed to come.

Who?

Sustain.

Breathe.

Love.

Give.

Live.

Learn.

Hurt.

Burn.

Share.

Growth.

Care.

...ing for her and him and he and she and we and they and them and me.

Close enough to appear further than where we are in actuality.

Who are we?

Who are we?

Really?

Who are we?

Contentment

Thoughts on paper

Pen onto page

Such anarchic forms of communication

Late night Thai

Early morning Japanese

These early morning faces look like early morning leaves, in a space on a tree where its branches no longer bear good fruit

Precipitation causes the branches to dissipate and then crumble right before my eyes

I hold out my hand to catch the residue of a falling twig

It misses me

And although it misses me, it blows in the wind and somehow kisses me

I wouldn't have had it any other way

Hollow Dreams

My bones are chilled, and not from the cold winter breeze.

My skin is layerless.

The thick dermaterial has eroded away along with passive-aggressive behavior, bitter-free emotions, and practical patterns of habitual practices done in the name of love.

What is it that I am looking for? I ask myself.

I visualize myself on a prairie, a wide-open field.

I imagine the greatest feeling ever felt by (wo)man.

I drift off into a deep sleep.

I have hollow dreams.

Scared of Lonely

It's funny how happy one can be when they're so busy that they don't even have time to think

In fact, it's the time you have to yourself that forces you to slow down and think that makes you feel sad and lonely

It's the beat that's in our chests that make us know that it's barely our breathing that we control

A body full of vessels and a hollow frame to a soul

A healing from a feeling will never truly be made whole

But that is what we fear most

Not our inability to grow, but in knowing that we will

We are unsure of the direction that we may go

We are unsure of the selection that God as the essence of the universe has made as our goals

So we are tearing down the posts and chopping down the poles

Feeling around in the dark for a purpose that may or may not be our own

Searching for an investment that won't land us near the throne

But scared of lonely is what we are and who we have come to be

It don't matter about tomorrow as long as today, lonely don't come for me

It's a punishment to ourselves and a curse for being unfaithful to our dreams

Unrealistic habitats always fade away with human tact

Unemotional and unimpassioned revenue is generated from a mindset that money can buy you happiness and a good life with a limited skillset

Nobody works to live yet everybody lives to work, but the fruits of their labor are more menial than mineral-less dirt

A dried-up representation of what can be perceived as real

Another illusion; blind the people who are already led astray by blasphemous confusion

Scared of Lonely

It's what we are and who we'll be, until we find our way

To be open...

My willingness to be open...

I feel as if others take me for granted

A state of mind that will someday return to attack me

I simply pray that my openness won't hurt me

Sanity

What gives to worry and angst about something that you cannot change?

Why dwell upon the past?

It will only eat you up on the inside

A raw new frame of mind and a piece of me that I reject is the piece that makes me free

Openness...

Sometime I hate it, but that's just *me*.

Face

Pieces of me scattered across the floor

I leave my heart on the board where I rested my head before I walk out the front door

Painting pictures of my future on the walls of my mind

Feeling remnants of forever off of the ceilings and tiles of time

Self-Savior

Maybe, just maybe, I'm saving someone who felt like me when asked how I was feeling and I said a little melancholy, but after my response I realized that I was downright depressed.

An in-denial, loveless sorrowful, suicidal wreck. Can't nobody tell me what I'm feeling ain't real. I'm having vasovagal syncope because my body shut down when my mind said to it, "I do not love you anymore."

Making excuses for a self that I did not create, abused by the men I love to hate but hating that I could not stop myself from loving them in return. I am jaded.

Fear and trembling falls upon me and I turn to a bottle that gets me faded when no one's around.

Forced to be a strong black woman but condemned by the anger I possess, capitulated by a society that bred me this way. I feel rage.

Tears fall down my face as I contemplate what it means to be a woman. Knowing that I may never have the ability to unmark my vulnerability, destigmatize my presence, or rectify my own shortcomings brings me falling to my knees.

Praying to God and yielding to my beliefs even when I feel sacrificially destructive. It's hard.

The pain burns inside me *verbatim* with the words that I speak to combat what others speak against me.

I'm tired.

I'm tired.

I'm tired.

But even when I'm tired, I somehow find the strength to live.

Maybe just maybe, I'm saving someone from themselves.

Solid Ground

Indigenous brothers and sisters, I stand with you
I weep in solidarity, in this red, white, and blue
They've made you invisible
But we know you exist
We know you're alive
We know you resist

Your oppression in this land precedes my ancestors' existence on
this continent
And like us, you're still fighting to be free
Up against government-sponsored environmental genocide ripping
through your communities

Standing Rock isn't the first act of resistance or movement on
Native ground from which you stand
But, I stand with you
It won't be the last in fracking chemicals and natural resources
for profit on the backs of the profitless on the sovereign land of a
sovereign nation
In any other part of the world, war would be waged and warranted
over libations

Native brothers and sisters, I stand with you
Both sympathetic and empathetic to your struggles

I know poverty and how it feels for the whole world to turn a blind
eye to your conditions
I know what it's like to only be recognized to the extent of
assimilation yet still get no recognition
I know not of my history from the lies I was taught in school
But from the burdens I have to carry, perceived as exceptional to
the rule

Storytellers of the soul, in honor and reverence, I stand with you
What's a native family to the red, white, and blue?
Paraphernalia and mascots
We know that's not who you are
They know not of your many cultures
And have no regard for the rituals under the stars

Tribal brothers and sisters, in love and respect, I stand with you
The winds are fast changing
My voice may not be heard afar
Just know, on the solid ground that links us all, I'm standing here
too

All lives, but black lives

You say that all lives matter, and I agree, but what of mine?

Sandra Bland. July 13, 2015. Hempstead, Texas.

You tell me I should not be divisive and align myself with those on only one side of the fence, but what of you Mr. and Mrs. Divide and Conquer?

Tamir Rice. November 22, 2014. Cleveland, Ohio.

You tell me to speak properly so that you can understand me, but you never seem to listen to the words that come out of my mouth.

Eric Garner. July 17, 2014. Staten Island, New York.

You tell me to watch my tone. My attitude and behavior, it feels too…free. No history of schizophrenia, but yet it is always read as erratic to you.

Tony Robinson. March 6, 2015. Madison, Wisconsin.

You tell me not to play the race card on a rigged floor of dealers shuffling out *black card revoked*, yet with no acknowledgement of my people or our contributions we are bought and sold as your commodity. Racial capitalism.

India Kager. September 5, 2015. Virginia Beach, Virginia.

You tell me to look presentable. You show me images to subscribe to because my beauty does not meet your standard, yet you pay to damage your skin cells to darken your tint and cornrow and loc your hair. You blow up your lips and hips, and replicate the Hottentot derriere.

Rekia Boyd. March 21, 2012. Chicago, Illinois.

Work hard like the rest of us, you say, but what of the unearned benefits you still receive from the New Deal? What of the tax breaks and incentives and transformative assets that built your new house upon the sturdy part of that hill?

Nicholas Thomas. March 24, 2015. Vinings, Georgia.

Stand up on your own two feet, you say, but then you break my kneecaps.

Freddie Gray. April 19, 2015. Baltimore, Maryland.

You acknowledge that bad apples are wrong, but what of the tree from which they were rung?

Bettie Jones. December 26, 2015. Chicago, Illinois.

What of the system of justice and fairness built on white supremacy and stratification?

Mike Brown. August 9, 2014. Ferguson, Missouri.

What of the perpetuation of a lack of awareness and consciousness, in exchange for food and shelter you have on loan to be bartered for bodily payments?

Alton Sterling. July 5, 2016. Baton Rouge, Louisiana.

What of the pro-black, but not synonymous and ignorantly mistaken to be anti-white, victims of cultural pilfering and economic deprivation?

What of the fractures in our skulls every time our heads hit the pavement?

Laquan McDonald. October 20, 2014. Chicago, Illinois.

What of our bravery for remaining civil during a war tugging on our souls?

And what of you, when *all lives* is the rhetoric but you're only accountable to your freedom?

Philando Castile. July 6, 2016. Falcon Heights, Minnesota.

And what of me, when my black life is lifeless and black bliss of blackness doesn't really matter?

Tanisha Anderson. November 13, 2014. Cleveland, Ohio.

Say their names!

Tyre King. September 14, 2016. Columbus, Ohio.

Say their names!

Yvette Smith. February 16, 2014. Bastrop, Texas.

Say their names!

Terence Crutcher, September 16, 2016. Tulsa, Oklahoma.

Say their names!

Aiyana Stanley-Jones. May 16, 2010. Detroit, Michigan.

Say their names, and have a seat!

Threat

For all the days you wake up with nothing but blackness on the spectrum of brown bodies, you will be perceived as a **threat**

Your three degrees and elite semicircles of the corner in which you sit give character and rise to **threat**

Your hands held high above your head in the air won't protect you from the implicit biases of those whom have deemed you **threat**

Your six languages and frequent travels around the world don't prevent you from feeling the weight of our brothers and sisters being gunned down in the streets and in their homes as **threats**

What is this crisis that polices the ways in which we call ourselves free? **Threat**

There can be no order or legitimacy for black bodies

Threat

Your conduct is discretionally made criminal as a function of order

Threat

Disorder is discretionally determined in need of lawful governance for bodies made criminal

Threat

The legitimacy of such systems that facilitate a process of order-maintenance depends on your subjugation to it

Threat

Requires your compliance and buy-in to a belief that you as an individual are responsible for the production of structural outcomes

Threat

"Broken Windows" are broken by design

Thr...

Paw Paw the Trailblazer in Mythical Form

I walked 978 miles from the South to the North barefoot with no understanding or concept of freedom

I just knew I wanted to be free

I labored eighteen hours in the strawberry fields of the Midwest while the only change in my pocket was the color of the lint as it dyed itself blue from the jeans wearing away at my crease

Didn't *no nigga* ever do shit for me

I got some mean ass memories, from the days of 108 degrees

Not to be confused with the education of the South that I didn't receive

Didn't *no nigga* ever do shit for me

I burned my britches and cashed in my niggary for a chance to hold the white man's hand and learn his trickery

I exposed my friends and the dirty secrets of my family

I never got the chance to know my grandmother cuz granddaddy shot her in the head on the plantation way back when

You see, way back then a black man's woman's pussy belonged to anybody who wanted it

He accused her of cheating

Didn't *no nigga* ever do shit for me

Born during an era of Crows safeguarding white men waving a flag of confederacy, I bred myself in a Northern state of democracy

I bore my cross and took my stride with a multitudinous appeal. Who needs to be humble when you got pride?

Embodying a sense of self of no black man before me

I was the *him* and the *him* was me

So don't talk that shit to me because didn't *no nigga* ever do shit for me

Over fifty years later and I got my own

I own two businesses and a congregation full of souls

My kids are lazy, but fuck em, they grown

Never seen they seedlings, no grandbabies that I call my own

Hell, they only call when in need and cry up on the phone

Curse me in their sleep and in their homes

But I don't got a Washington for no muthafuckin George that can't find a Weezy to wipe his ass clean

Didn't *no nigga* ever do shit for me

I say...

Didn't *no nigga* ever do shit for me

Strange Fruit, yet oh so familiar

Strange fruit, yet oh so familiar
From whence do you grow?
How far did you travel?
Tell me, I must know

What is the metaphor for tree and noose in your language of today?
I see your body swinging and legs dangling in my mind as I kneel
to pray

Strange fruit, yet oh so familiar
Do you hear me? I'm talking to you
Playing Billie Holiday and Nina Simone in the background on vinyl,
yet for some reason our eras bring us here together in truth
To the place where bloody leaves have been dyed permanently red
from the root
And the crop is creamier than the year before, and certainly richer
than the day before last

This strange fruit is not so strange anymore
Negro spirituals memorializing burning flesh piping hot can be
heard running through black churches and living room doors
Seeking to escape the darkness
Hoping for an intervention to even the score

This fruit, most familiar to the arms of capitalism, is essential for a profitable neoliberal state

Necessary to be *hanging* as a spectacle of inferiority and made criminal to a law enforced by no law-abiding citizens

Gangbanging domestic terrorists supreme reign through structured discourse, and policies and practices and nexuses

Freedom is an illusion captivated by the mind

Bred to teach me that the alternative to being strange fruit is a vegetable. Pun intended.

My dearest strange fruit
Do you recognize yourself?
What are the material conditions of your root?
Do you know even know that you're strange fruit?

"6"

Sitting on the edge of my mother and father's bed, I could hear the water trickling from the faucet of the porcelain tub in the bathroom nearby. It was my mother's sweet escape from him, and us. My eyes were glued to the television screen; my right leg dangling from the left side of the mattress. I wondered what it would be like to be a white woman as I sat gazing into the big beautiful blue eyes of Joan Crawford on the box in front of me. A movie, made way before my time, yet felt so relevant. Her fictitious world, eons away from mine, provided imagination that stimulated a mental safe haven of sorts. I watched as she dragged on a cigarette in between lines. I looked down into my father's ashtray sitting on the nightstand beside the bed and grabbed a butt to imitate her beauty. Casually, I began to play house with myself. "Oh darling," I said as I put the cigarette butt to my mouth pretending to smoke, "What brings you here today?" I belched in an awkwardly childish English accent. "I didn't think…" My father grabbed my hand. I froze. I was so lost in my world that I did not hear him coming up the stairs. "Soooo you want to smoke?" he yelled. "Huh?" he shouted even louder as he snatched me off the edge of the bed and shook my entire body. I tried to look past him to Joan on the screen. There was no clapperboard for this moment in time. No *cut* or accolades for my performance like there was in Joan's movies. "You wanna fuckin smoke? Let's smoke!" He grabbed a pack of Newport Shorts out of his pocket and opened the top for me to pull. "Nuh…" I mumbled as I started to cry. "Noooo. I'm sorry. I don't wanna smoke."

"Stop fuckin crying. You were just pretending to smoke." I stood at four feet with my back now facing the TV. I could still hear Joan in the background, but the only face I could see was his. Brows furrowed and mean. I had made him angry. He grabbed my tiny fingers and made me pull six cigarettes out of his pack. "Maaaaaaaaaaaa," I screamed. "Moooooooooom."

"Why are you yelling for her? She can't help you!" He was right. She couldn't. She was in the bathroom directly across from the bedroom with the door wide open and didn't make a sound. I could hear my two older brothers creeping up the stairwell only to peek into the bedroom to see what was going on. No one dared to stop him. My eyes welled up as I watched them peeking their heads through the doorway in silence, trying to remain invisible to him. He shoved several cigarettes in my mouth and lit them all at once. After a few sobbing drags, I spit them all out onto the floor in coughing rage. "Is your throat dry?" he asked as he handed me a half-empty forty-ounce bottle of Old English. I shook my head no. "Drink it!" I kept coughing. "Now." He pushed the bottle into my chest. "And you're going to stand there until it's finished." I drank. He picked up the cigarettes off the floor and pushed them back into my mouth. "Smoke." I smoked. He sat back on the bed watching with a smirk on his face. The voices on the screen behind me began to fade away along with my childhood. Playing house was not a game in my reality. I even stopped crying. My tears were not needed here. When I got down to the bottom of the bottle, my stomach erupted. I dropped everything and ran into the bathroom across the hall. "Ahhhhh," I screamed as I threw up what felt like all of my undeveloped organs. I began to sob with my head bent over in the toilet. I tilted my head toward my mother sitting in the tub. My eyes said, *why*. She only gazed back at me with an unmoving, helpless stare. My sadness turned to anger, more so at her than him. I was angry that she wasn't strong enough to save me; disappointed that she couldn't find the power to save herself. I cleaned myself up. I buried my face in the towel on the rack as she buried her head between her legs propped up near her chest in the tub. I shut the door on my way out. At six, I was going on sixteen.

Reflections from Stateville at Stateville

At Stateville. In class. I'm staring at a poster on a cupboard with a picture of Garfield and Odie that reads "Welcome to class. You may think now." Hmmm…interesting how as you enter the classroom you are given permission to think, as if you weren't able to think outside of the classroom setting. As if you don't have a brain, a mind of your own, and thoughts within this modern-day institution of slavery. As if you are led like sheep among a herd with many shepherds as blind as you are socialized to be. The classroom screamed *this is where the learning begins* with 8½ by 11 sheets of paper with colorful images shaded with crayons plastered on uninterrupted blue walls of silence.

Within the prison walls I stood to the right of every hallway of the employee entrance. My eyes clung to the walls as I stared at framed photos of gates and technosecurity apparatuses sending a message to all passersby (employee, volunteer, or visitor) that surveillance, security, and consequence reign. Visual images designed to incite mental and physical stimulation so that you instantly become aware that even you are being watched. Your nerves are sending messages to your brain, giving you a heightened sense of awareness that tells you that you should be alert…more aware of bodies being regulated by the structure they dwell within.

Shakedown at the entrance. Photo ID at every gate. Small talk from the men and silence from the women *in charge*. I asked to use the restroom when the instructor directed me to "ask the security guard." Before I could open my mouth to speak, the correctional officer approached me swiftly, and angrily asked, "Did she just call me a security guard?" I paused. "Ummm, I don't really know," I responded. "I am *not* a security guard, *We* are correctional officers," she retorted. Not sure how to respond, I replied, "I'll be sure to let her know." To which she responded, "Oh don't worry, I *will*," screaming back at me. It took everything inside of me not to laugh in her face before she stormed off in the direction of the instructor. My only thought was this: does not a security guard and a correctional officer serve the same purpose? After all, they are merely eyes on the street (in this case, on the yard), purposed to maintain obedience and regulate social behavior. She was angry. She was aggressive. She is a pawn in this game of chess. A low-level player in this game of life. I took note of her sex and the way in which she performed her gender...authoritative, hypermasculine behavior. Her position was one that demanded respect. The inmates recognized their position and knew their places, recreating a stable environment not only physically but mentally, spiritually, and emotionally as well.

I close my eyes and all I can see are mental replications of a cafeteria. Frequent chowtime riots ensue the use of lethal force. Stood up? *Sit down.* First shot into the white box. *Gun lowered.* Second shot into the room. *Gun aimed at an inmate.* Third shot with intent to wound, possibly kill. More mutiny? *Tear gas released from the ceilings and walls debilitating everyone trapped in the room.* Lockdown. One shower a week unless you have a job. 28 cents an hour for the employed. Toothpaste. Deodorant. $270 for 13-inch TVs. $35 for fans.

...slavery. Flesh-filled mechanical robots. Powered on and operated by heavy-duty machinery. I too must participate. *Powered off.* "Gate open," the correctional officer yelled. I walked through gates and doors. As they close behind me, I have an option to return. Single file out of the prison. Off of the lawn. Visitor badge removed. I'm back to the cave of life beyond bars.

Break Free

Stubborn are the kinks of my hair and the ways of my people standing tall with long legs screaming Africa.

An image so profane yet beautifully created, the obscene nudity of our bodily forms birthed art.

Slang mastered by the chain gang knew no Ebonics, only familiar words being spoken.

Trade a nigga in for a college degree, exchange broken English for old English and you got yourself a recipe for token.

Can you stay awake long enough to feel the vibration of my vocals on the beating drum clogging up your ears?

Or are you an insomniac during mayhem?

A spinning dreidel, barely able to function and contain yourself from the societal drama that's pulling you under?

Under a tideless tide, musical theory's last composition *be* noted a hood anthem.

Mismatched colors patched together to make an uncoordinated design. It wasn't cool until the coolest kids on the block rocked skulls and crossbones on their skirts, belt buckles, and kicks.

Righteous.

Little black boys and girls can now rock out to rock stars like Stevie Nicks, as long as you got a hot beat master on the track, maybe a trapper giving back.

Platinum pocketing millions not giving a dime to the community where they shot a video vigilizing the struggle.

Great black leaders can only lead us until they themselves have gone astray.

We praise the corruption and turn away from those who have negatively acted or reacted out of frustration toward a system that has failed you.

On any level, the Prince of Peace has a golden key to release your grief on an ascending stairway to heaven.

Those of you who chose the latter, please remove your ladder so that the rest of us can begin to step in the name of love.

I see you making motions like you're torn between devotion and loyalty to a house that ain't quite your home.

But your confusion has perpetuated more than an illusion, *this* home is where the hatred is.

Evasive situationless decisions can't be valued when the basis is greed and hate.

I don't have to worry about misidentifying with you because your constructed identity was a mistake.

A patterned process of practice makes permanent, *you* went against your fate.

Freewheeled a path, but you blame your own and only you can help yourself escape.

So, break free my brother. Break free, my sister.

Break free!

Same Race. Different Politics.

We share the same race,
Yet we're cut from a woolly fabric of different politics.

Black bodies existing in a space in which they're already dead is
something on which we can agree,
Yet you suppress my voice with your sexist gender-stereotyped
coded language that contrives projected emotion and pathologizes
the rationale that justifies your refusal to hear me speak.

We both share a common language of black English,
Yet our dialects are not one and the same.
My womanist, feminist constructions of identity and approaches to
inquiry are discomforting to your taste.
It is clear that my dialectical expressions of intellectualism and self
have no place on your multidimensional complex palette of race
through a hypermasculine lens of manhood.

Our hair is coarse.
Our noses are wide.
Our mothers love hard.
Our fathers abandoned us. We have daddy issues as a result.
Our communities are barren. It wasn't our fault.
Our families are familiar with addiction. Addicts have impacted
our lives.

Our brothers have been swallowed by the criminal legal system. We are kindred slaves as enemies of the state.

Our belief is in education. We know it affords us opportunity but access is no guarantee.
Our skin is the color of mocha. We call ourselves black.
Our hearts are broken. Love always leaves us behind but leaves a trail for us to find.
Our faith is unwavering. Though we often are critical of God.

Yet your interactions with me are oppressive, and divisive in nature.
Sadly, you probably aren't even aware.
Questioning the validity of my thoughts and contributions.
Insulting and demeaning at the juncture at which you do not agree.
Adopting the strategies of those whom you critique.
Using the master's tools...
Not to dismantle the master's house,
But as a weapon against people who look like you.
Dividing and conquering your way through battle.

Your fight isn't with me. I am not your enemy, black man.
Until you wake up and realize *that* we'll forever be worlds apart, living in the same skin.
You can't claim to be "woke" if you turn a blind eye to the suffering of your own women, especially when there is blood on your own hands.

Yet and still, I love you!

Worst Secret

We were both as youthful as the wooden playground that engulfed us, though he much older than I. Holding hands, my body slouched next to his. The summer leaves rustled about. His soul was just as gentle and cool as the breeze that hugged my arms and legs. "You're beautiful!" he whispered as he stroked my leg. Though an unanticipated silence, there was never a dull moment between us.

"How many wooden pieces do you think it took to make this playground?" I asked.

"359."

"Ah, so definitive. How can you be so sure?" I said, laughing.

"Well, it's not hard to figure out when the masterpiece is right in front of you." He smiled. I smiled back.

"I'm gonna say it took about seven trees to make this thing." He burst into laughter.

Why seven?

"It's the number of completion." It was no coincidence that it was Sunday.

"Hmm."

"What? Don't act like you weren't raised in the church!"

"No, I was. Four-hour services, chicken dinners, and everything."
We both laughed. Our conversations were always familiar territory.

"I don't think any church service should ever be that long, unless
it's a wedding or something big." I said. "Yeah, I don't want my
wedding to be that long." My eyes lit up.

"Oh yeah? And just how long do you want it to be?" My tone
reduced to a sweet voice somehow unfamiliar to myself.

"Well, it's going to be about two and half hours, tops. I'm not
paying for a minute longer." He looked down and smiled at me. I
rolled my head into the contour of his neck.

"Well, it seems like you've got it all figured out. I thought only little
girls fantasize about their weddings." I teased and pulled back to see
just how serious he was.

"Stereotype." He said. "That happens to be true." We laughed. I
playfully pushed him. "Seriously, I've given it some thought. It's not
a fantasy." he said.

"Oh!" My heart started racing. Excitement bubbled up in my
stomach. Palms began to get moist beneath the wing of the wind.
My fingers tingled.

He grabbed both of my hands as he gently pulled me in to face him.
I can't get married now, I thought to myself. *Ooooh, what's happening
here? I love him. He's so amazing but I just graduated high school. What
about college? He's already gone to college. My wild oats have not been
sown.*

"Are you still there?" he said, softly poking fun to get my attention. I snapped out of my daydream.

"Uh, yeah! Sorry. What were you saying?"

"I'm getting married!" My eyes grew wide. I think I may have stopped breathing. My voice shaking as I struggled to catch my breath, I said, "Ooooh!"

And on day seven, of the seventh day of the month, in the seventh month of the year, whatever imagined love affair I thought we were having had suddenly come to an end.

Connection

Connection.

We're always seeking connection.

Without it, you're lost.

We've been brainwashed, indoctrinated.

To repeat, regurgitate an idea that we are all ruled by logic.

And maybe not all of us because of the ways in which we are structured to be divided.

Men must conquer all.

We are taught that men are ruled by logic.

And women are ruled by emotion.

But the limbic region in our brains connect nerves, fluids, glands, and ventricles, releasing chemicals and endorphins for us to feel.

There can be no relationship or connection without feeling.

There is no logic to love.

There is no strategy to opening up your heart and sacrificially extending a part of you that you did not know existed until the moment that you felt...different.

Connection.

How is it that I'm supposed to find the partner of my life or the individual of my dreams, when I can connect emotionally but not sexually; sexually by not spiritually; spiritually but not mentally; mentally but not metaphysically? How can we connect?

Connection.

Like blue and red chips, sliding down a plastic instrument.

Seeking to line up in a row. You only need four to win.

And if there is a blue on top of a red, or a red in between a blue that disconnects you from your ability to be able to connect...four.

It disconnects you from your ability to connect...more.

It disconnects you from being able to breathe outside of that context.

I tell him, I feel hurt. I feel pain. I feel like you don't love me. I feel like you don't listen. I feel like you don't show me care. I feel like you don't understand me.

He responds, "That's just your *feeling*. It's the way you *feel*. And just because it's the way that you *feel* doesn't make it right. It doesn't make it real. It doesn't make it true. It doesn't make it... my problem. Because I'm concerned with what is real."

But what's real is how I feel. What's real is my reality. What I feel is my perspective, which shapes my life. My life is how I'm able to connect with others who are moving through time simultaneously on top of words and phrases and thoughts and notes.

People who think in color. People who think in black and white. Our ability to connect impacts all of that. It shapes everything that we don't even understand has form.

Connection is who we are.

Connection is what we know.

Connection is all we'll ever be.

Wordplay

Working on becoming humbly considerate

I used to be an arrogant, inconsiderate, cynical *muhfuka*

I didn't care what you thought or how you felt

Fuk ya feelings with ya mind

I didn't give a damn about being the help

Except to those feeling marginalized by a greater oppressor seeking to silence them

Yet I silenced them by my ability to say more than the next, and much more than the one who spoke before me

Wordplay

It was rare when I actually had something to say, but I liked the way that my ideas could roll off my tongue like an octave assignment in a choral position

I was fascinated by my ability to recreate my own sentence transition

Wordplay

I had words for days and sentences for hours

It didn't matter what others had to say

Fuk em, I could give you word showers

I used to be voiceless

A being that was silenced

Only the pen and paper could express how I viewed the violence

…how the violence viewed me

Chasing a feeling that would never be felt if conversations could be complete

And open dialogue could be that tweet

But in the heart of our home, the children were just the seed

No eyes to see

No lips to speak

No ears to hear

You better pretend that they are all invisible because no one cared to know that they were there

So yes, I grew up, and every chance that I got I opened up my mouth to what my mind was thinking

Thank God I never got popped, the drunken words had me sinking

Wordplay

Working on becoming humbly considerate

I used to be an arrogant, inconsiderate, cynical *muhfuka*

No feelings, no emotions, and I'd write a poem to sing my cover

As I prayed to become a humble individual, I realized that my actions made people victim to meta forms of oppression all while I preached liberation, exposing race, gender, and class oppression

I began to realize that the sensory receptors understood more than what my play on words had idealized to perfection

Watching how others reacted, how responses were faint, and how people zoned out when I spoke even when I had something to say

They didn't know the difference

Since I always had something to say, being radical to them was merely a radical existence...a distance that they began to put between me and them

Damn, I do care about your contribution

We have to work together

But I put my foot in my mouth too early, and the riders that I needed had left my ship

My consciousness was still lifted, but the lesson had to be built

The (wo)man that knows something knows that (s)he knows nothing at all

Wordplay

Listening. Learning. Observing.

Wordplay

Feeling. Hurting. Burning.

Wordplay

South Texas

Today I met a woman whom with piercing eyes has endured much suffering.

The beauty of her youth looked as if it were never fading, but for her consisted of a pain that stung from her heart to her tongue.

Donación? Donación? Donación?

…is what she cried. She spoke. I listened.

Her broken English filled the atmosphere resounding louder than her tears.

Spanish is what she spoke to me in a way that I never knew that I could understand.

Not knowing what to say, my spirit moved before my mind and I reached out to touch her hand.

With my other hand, I reached for my purse and then into my wallet.

What's a dollar to a blessing walking testimonial remission with a hole in her heart but a penny for her living? When you think about it, when all is said and done, life is nothing without giving.

When she touched my hand and looked in my eyes, I could see down into her soul.

Before she opened her mouth, her tears told a story of a pain so hot and intense yet her words could melt the cold.

Off in the distance sat two little boys singing underneath a desert tree.

"Mis dos hijos. Quiero lo mejor," is what she whispered to me.

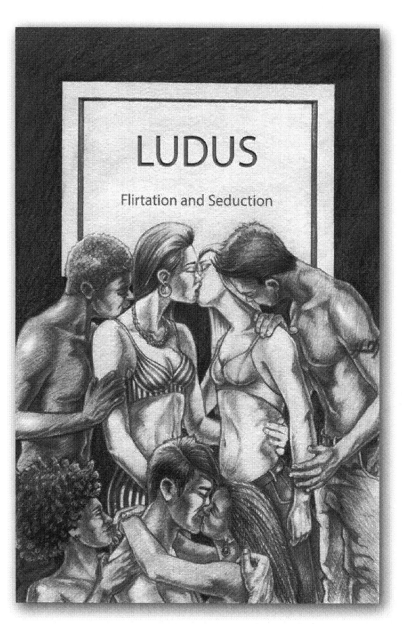

LUDUS

Flirtation and Seduction

This pussy was not made for your dicking

I know your mother told you that you were God's greatest gift to Earth.

That even Adam as first man in the Garden of Eden and Noah being chosen to preserve the species wasn't tantamount to your birth.

But *this pussy* was not made for your dicking.

Washed every tear you ever had, allowing you to hide your emotions in the shadows.

The phrase "be a man" was a euphemism for *no need to work through your emotions like an ordinary human being because one day some woman will be so happy to have a man that they'll happily take on the burden of my baby.*

Telling you that a woman who doesn't tolerate your shit must be crazy.

Yet *this pussy* was not made for your dicking.

With your fine ass, radiating of melanin and the Jergens you substituted for Old Spice.

Occupying those colonizing features that still make combating colorism a relevant fight.

Texting me in the mornings and late into the night.

Copy and pasting what you sent to her so I'd be reminded that I'm still on your mind.

This pussy was not made for your dicking. Sweetheart, you're wasting your time.

You pay for dinner and two rounds of drinks.

Then you want to get frisky?

I've kept you out past your bedtime, now you want to get busy.

Asking me if we can go to a theatre near my place so you can get closer to these sheets.

Thinking you're stimulating by warming up my thighs and cheeks with the heat from your leather seats.

So you bought me flowers. Spent a few nights on the phone.

Opened up a couple doors. And dropped me off at home.

You hit me with your best shot. Make your request, though in your mind it's a given.

And when I politely decline your offer, you ask me if I'm into women?

No, my dear friend, *this pussy* just ain't made for your dicking.

Oh yes, how could I forget? You've just spent $83.49.

But your currency gives my labia no urgency to open the doors of this temple.

Throwing your cheap penis around for the price of nothing will not add value to the thrust of simple.

Perhaps if your mind was just as complex as this complex below, I'd be interested in your heavish dickery fever.

Perhaps if you cared to listen when I described my character you'd be a little less eager.

Independence, intelligence, and intellectualism are not synonymous for ignorance.

So your unfettered fetish for my attributes to say you *came* and conquered requires a bit more diligence.

Sorry to disappoint, though I'm sure you have others primed for your picking.

But *this pussy* right here?

Ha!

Certainly wasn't made for the pleasure of your dicking.

Attraction

All of the faces look the same.

Black fades to brown as brown fades to black.

Stenciled eyes and ears, much has been drawn to make a face.

Penciled in with permanent ink. The only hope of erasing the lining now is with *Wite-Out*.

How can we do-over a mistake that was always meant to be?

The lines look complete and are obviously in need of correction.

No new ideas?

No more birthmarks.

Beauty is for the birthless.

Lust

Murmuring lips are all starting to sound the same to me.

Vague charismatic expressions convey messages of sweet somethings, but they're really saying nothing of value.

There is no meaning to the words that roll off their tongues.

It's where *like* becomes a synonym for love and *love* becomes a high-strung rhythm on a note without a beat.

Praying to the heavens.

I lift my heart to you.

Didn't have to know his name to know that he wasn't from you.

No Drama, No Bias, No Bullshit!

Just representing an irreparable era.

Smiley faces in the sand but no face to make for hand-to-hand, just a concentrated powder granulated like raw sugar cane.

If what I say is fiction then it's a riddle, but if I state a fact then please believe my story will have more chords and strings than a fiddle.

A working masterpiece is what the world must be.

A pure distraction of personal interactions introduced by what we call technology.

No conversation needed just to pull down your pants.

And if the first time is good then I'll give you a second chance.

But no drama, no bias, no bullshit.

Chase

I'm chasing pavements

Although the cement is still dying, but in the open sun

I'm facing pavements

A lump of emotions

Pinching my nerves and sending signals to my brain

I could scream at the top of my lungs but the top of my lungs would be the bottom of yours because you don't waste much breath on me

I often question myself on the illusion of time because Ms. Timeless Existence missed her scheduled appointment

Merely existing without the constraints of time, she is fascinated

Memories

Memories.
She sits...and waits in a place unbeknownst to herself, an unfamiliar
setting to her surroundings. Her fetal consciousness goes "tap tap
tap" on her uterine door.
She spreads her wings and remembers back to a time when her
feathers were teased by *his* golden trumpet.

Memories.
In a room with cold, hard tiling and plastic stirrups, the metal from
the frozen bedframe burned her dried-cummed thighs.
Incisions, scars, and scabs marked her yearning obsession to be
cleansed.

Each wash was more futile than the last.
What once was an innocent kitty was now a bad pussy smelling of
saliva dripped 211 and Newport shorts.
No minty aftermath from the menthol as carcinogens and strands
of mononucleosis and streptococcus bacteria find their way to a
new home.
Housed inside her endometrial lining are new cells and bigger than
the one downstate that holds what's left of *him*.

She sits...and waits in a place unbeknownst to herself, an unfamiliar
setting to her surroundings. Her fetal consciousness goes "tap tap
tap" on her uterine door.

A stain on the wall takes her back to the day when her once-white dress was dyed red, and as it dried it quickly turned maroon.

"I'll give you flowers for your garden," he promised as he violently drained his pipe down the gutter of her own garden.
He moistened her soil, too stupid to understand that when you plant and water a seed, it must grow.
He was too fucked up to care.

Memories...a faint distorted imagery of past realities.
She closes her eyes ever so often to understand if what she is experiencing real.
Psoriasis on her fingertips wore away her sense of being able to feel...internal pain.
Malignantly experiencing a benign tumor of pain, no emotions wreak havoc because she feels as if she has brought this upon herself.
Soft eyes, pretty face, thin waist, thick thighs, and natural kinky dark brown hair that the motherland gave as a gift to complement her beauty.
Desiring to be closer to her ancestral ties, she felt the normalcy of lying down and taking it was her duty.
As she rests her head on the pillow and her back to the bed, she drifts off while staring at tiny holes in the ceiling.
...remembering back to the days before *he* gave her tiny pink hole feeling.

Memories.
She spreads her wings once more, but she is far too weak to fly.

Soft tears run down her face but she does not know if it is the physical pain of the suction pump or her...memories.

Flashing lights begin to strobe across her closed eyelids as her adrenalized thoughts began to flow. I only smiled and said hello, she softly cried.

I only knew him for three weeks so I told him *no*.

He told me that I could be the Eden of his garden.

A place where serpentless fruit and vegetables can grow and not become a victim of wisdomless symptomatic jargon.

Although I'm guilty of opening up my heart to him, I never gave him permission to violate my temple.

All of the lies that I was taught about avoiding peer pressure and *just saying no*, it just wasn't that simple.

Memories.

No. Memories. *No.* Memories. *No.* Memories. *Ok.* Memories. *Maybe.* Memories. *Yeah.* Memories. *I guess.* Memories. *No.* Memories. *Stoooop.* Memories.

She sits...and waits in a place unbeknownst to herself, an unfamiliar setting to her surroundings. Her fetal consciousness goes "tap tap tap" on her uterine door.

She attempts to spread her wings but they are broken.

Her halo is tarnished, but her spirit levitates and removes from her body the last breath of mumbled words being spoken.

She makes her carnal exit, and like her memories, she is now a faint distorted imagery of past realities.

Memories.

Amerikkka, you're a terrible boyfriend!

They told me you were amazing
With you, I could lose myself and be free
You'd protect from all wrongdoings
You'd help me to be anything I wanted to be

I got a slick tongue but they told me not worry
Bill is open-minded with his *Rights*
He's as progressive as they come
Comparing him to other men is like confusing day and night

He loves an independent woman, they say
One who can stand on her own two feet
One who is highly educated and redefines feminism
One who won't back down and cave into defeat

He's such a free-spirit individual now, they told me
Hell, his eldest son is gay
He's Christian but his best friends are Muslim
He and black people go way back in the day

He's incredibly supportive of immigrants
Just you wait, watch, and see

You've never met a man like him before, they told me
You'll fall in love with the man they call *Democracy*

My girl, she set me up
Gave me your number, I gave you a call
You wined and dined me for weeks
As far as I could tell, they were right about all

You made me feel so good at first
Told me that you didn't mind me having a job
Didn't mind me being educated
As long as I supported you and your cause

You didn't mind me speaking my mind
As long as I did it respectfully
You didn't mind me disagreeing
As long as I didn't organize others collectively

That honeymoon stage was great
After all, I respected all your wishes
You incentivized my loyalty
Adorned me with a taste of your riches
But then I had a taste of my own blood
After you pummeled me in the kitchen

You said that you were sorry
That you would not do it again
But when my girls confronted you about it
You took your violence out on my friends

They told me that I needed to leave you
But, I have nowhere to go
You are the only home I've ever known
The only place I felt *free* to grow

You told me that I was disrespectful for not allowing you to treat
me that way
That I should've been more than grateful to have a man willing to
throw a few scraps my way

You told me that you owned me
And that I should never forget my debt to you
You made it clear that the price could be paid with my life
In spite of my fortitude

What about all of the things you promised me?
All of the *dreams* you put inside my head?
I believed you really loved me
I believed we'd grow old together
I believed that you had changed
That you no longer had the capacity to be fair-weather

I'm writing you from a shelter that resembles a camp with those
whom you've thought best to contain
But even in containment the people around me still refuse to believe
the things they've seen of you
They still think you're better than what people are saying

But, I've spent a lot of time with you
And I certainly know the truth
The man you've finally shown yourself to be
Is the real man inside of you…

Hateful
Violent
Malicious and unaccepting
Disloyal
Destructive
Deceitful and unloving

Amerikkka, you're a terrible boyfriend!
We don't have to keep pretending…

EROS

Sex

Passion

Romance

Bold, Brown, Beauty

Honeysuckle, melon dew, a cantaloupe, a kiss from you is worth a thousand words.

A mumble from your quivering lips makes me speechless to speak phrases that may be unclear when heard by your ears.

A delightful beauty is your moonshine as I become intoxicated by your positive energy and desire.

I only drink in moderation. I do not believe in consuming in excess but the overindulgence of your love has me in an ultimate state of bliss and temptation, not wanting to deny the fruit that you could someday give to me.

Bold, Brown, Beauty. An essence of everlasting you are. Your soft medium-brown eyes light up the room in *mon coeur.*

A murmur you gave me when you whispered my name. You sheltered yourself within the walls of my atrium and made a bed in *ma chambre.*

You sealed my hole with a passion that no ultrasound can see, hear, nor detect.

I fear vulnerability, a space where freedom is only free as long as we abide by its rules and guidelines.

A perfect place for a new beginning, a start all over with you.

Beautiful you are...

Bold, Brown, Beauty. An essence of everlasting you are...poetry.

How Can I Define Us?

How can I define us?

It's just the gravity, of our inner energy coming together

How can I define us?

Other than our spirits flying free

Your soul connects your heart to me

Our love's forever

Love is a Verb!

Love is a verb
And not just any verb, but an action verb
A verb that requires you to "do," to "act"
A verb that encourages you to "be" better

Love is a verb
A love language often unfulfilled
An expression often misunderstood
The neurotransmitters that reside in our brains before signaling our hearts to follow

Love is a verb
A chain reaction of goodness that shows how much you care
The presence of your mind and body to indicate you're there
A gesture of romance and affection when you don't have a dime to your name
Showing up without being requested simply because you know they'll be glad you came

Love is a verb
Not just a feeling
Or a channel of worthless words rolling off your tongue for good measure

Because they smile when they hear you say it, giving you the self-satisfaction of pleasure

Love is...

I Desire

If I could scribe a message to you in a bottle it would say, "I love you."

Expression.

If I knew how to calligraphy the art of hieroglyphics as a poem for you to read the life of my struggle, I would tell you that I need you.

Expression.

If I knew the dance of my ancestors and the song of my people, I would cry out in my native tongue, "I want you."

Expression.

Hello. I am a victim of cultural molestation.

I desire.

Imposter

Sometimes love can break you down

Make you feel less than and inadequate

Unloved

Unforgiving

Wait!

That's not love...

What is Love?

Where is the only place that you will not find Love? Someone asked me.

In our hearts, I replied.

In the bellies of our souls dancing on the bottomless floor that holds our beliefs and carries our faith will you find Love.

What is Love?

Is it a decree-pumping vessel victoriously pulsating to produce a pure and honest feeling?

Do we elicit feelings of hope and sacrifice simply as a result of this?

Love is what we believe, maybe what we don't.

We make decisions with our mind and kindly ask our hearts to follow.

Essentially, we give our hearts permission to invite a detrimental feeling or series of hazardous emotions down for tea and crumpets.

But there is no trumpet sounding of joy in a ride that will walk you right into the perils of loneliness and heartbreak.

Love.

You never can know. This humanly constructed word for a Godly inspired ethereal concept.

We feel it, and we don't know what it is, so we call it Love.

We experience it, and we don't have the ability to explain it, so we call it Love.

Love.

What really is Love?

For all we know, this universal feeling that we share could not really be Love at all.

Bleeding Walls

As paint drops down these walls, the window frames begin to melt away with the pain growing in my heart and stirring up confusion in my soul.

Plates shifting places on the ceiling as opposed to underneath the ground.

Tectonic movements cut life but can't be washed away like bones disintegrating upon the earth, but somehow that domino effect will always find you first.

Whispers beneath the shadows. I pray *yea, though I walk through the valley of the shadow of death*, couldn't be much more than death itself.

…yet still I fear no evil.

These whispers in the dark turn into music in the park and I'm dancing to a beautiful love song, clinging on to a silhouette of a love to come and rescue me.

PRAGMA

Understanding
Compatibility
Compromise

The Unimaginary

Some people will never be what you what them to be, but they'll always be who they are.

They may never do what you want them to do, but they always do what they feel.

Some wait their whole lives for the potential to unravel and unfold.

And sometimes, it does.

Most times, not in the way that one might imagine.

Perhaps the imagination is something unimagined as well.

Perhaps it isn't.

Either way, a life less giving isn't worth being explored.

Meenah Mae

There was no communication.

And the words that were communicated were like lead, in paint, discrete to the naked eye but when tasted by the buds of a soft, sweet tongue it produces poison.

Toxic toxins growing from the pit of her stomach, she upchucked arson.

Hoping that the fire from her words burned him worse than her inflamed cervix.

Misery is what she felt for loving the company that she kept.

Guilt arose within her for giving and being naïve to the possibility of ever receiving an unwrapped gift in return.

No receipts come with this return, and exchanges don't have a fourteen- or thirty-day policy, and the only expiration date is her last day on Earth.

Loving him unconditionally, she gave him all she had, while he gave her all that she had.

He was her husband.

With vows being taken for better or worse, her only exception was infidelity.

Her fragile heart couldn't bear the melody of him plucking the string of another guitar or stroking the keys of a less fine-tuned piano.

She clings to the air that he breathes.

As he breathes out air and in hallucinogens, disrupting his pathological disposition.

She used to be his heroine, now his only *she*ro is heroin, a bump of coke, a drink of gin to ease his nerves.

Calm his temper and pacify his desires.

He's now a liar.

Consistent and she's tired…of him telling her, "Baby, I'm gonna make it better."

She fixes what is broken, and he makes it wetter making it almost impossible to leave his world behind.

Our worlds aligned when she told me that she was leaving.

Had no more energy for the heathen that he hulked himself into.

Divorce.

Now she plans on walking away with kids in hand and a child-support check over a one-night stand.

He begs and pleads for her to stay.

The Race of Love

You stopped running because you could not see the finish line

But I was forced to stop because I ran out of time

Are you going to stop pursuing your dream because you cannot see into the future?

I thought not

We cannot forfeit now just because we are tired

I am just slowing for water

You are walking

You said that you are giving up and quitting the race because you have done all that you could

If you had done all that you could, then you would have continued running even after I slowed down

But you didn't

You began to walk instead, which makes us *both* entirely responsible losers for quitting the race

I never wanted to quit, so I volunteered to carry you on my back while you catch a breath

I will run

You only replied to me, "You will be running alone"

What great teamwork!

Monogamy

Monogamy isn't natural, but it's real if you really want it.

I don't believe the chastity hype about preserving yourself to be with that one extraordinary being for the rest of your life.

The lies that we're fed about love curing all desires, attractions, and proclivities to win the affections of others outside of your two-person unit.

The bible speak we digest and regurgitate to keep our households in order. Our labias friendless. Our scrotums cooler than the body.

Having to work tirelessly at keeping your loins burning for one, but cheating behind closed doors and lying in public to cover it up because our hearts are in the right places and emotions with the ones we love.

Can you imagine a world without the socialization of monogamy?

One without the narrative of a lifeless long-term commitment for sale, for all to invest despite the low rate of interest on the return.

A world in which people simply act and do according to how they conduct themselves in their natural settings.

Think about it! How might that change our conceptualization of love? Relationships? Identity? Partners?

How might it change our approach to life?

Living and breathing, excited to simply connect and be beautiful in the present. Not concerned with losing something good because the goodness bleeds through the moment.

Obviously, I don't believe monogamy is natural. However, I do believe that if you make a conscious decision to be in a committed relationship with one individual, you owe it to that person and yourself to be respectful enough to adhere to your commitment.

If not, perhaps monogamy is something you should reconsider.

AGAPE

The highest form of love
Unconditional
God, as the essence of the universe

Do You Know God?!

Do you know God?!

A question I've been asked time and time again.

As if God is this fictitious character frowning from a seat above with minions below.

Among a vast sea of ornaments that we call stars, hanging from the tree of life as we know it.

He reigns supremely they say, as if supreme beings have any other way of reigning...down on you.

Do you know God?

He is gentle. He is loving. He is gracious. He is tender. He is kind. He is sacrificial. He is forgiving. He has no ego. He does not boast. He is humble.

He...sounds...like...a woman.

I know no man who is all of the above at the same time.

Do you know God?

I read about *him* in church but *she* saved me in my home.

His work was praised in bible study but *her* allegiance got me into the room.

I sowed a good seed and reaped the essence of her harvest.

The universe responded accordingly.

When I started to understand my own energy, I met an omnipresent kinetic source that introduced me to myself.

Do you know God?
Made in her image.
My God, she left an impression.
The alpha and omega, but no finite measure marks the beginning or the end.
Her queerness is best understood in the deep discoveries of ourselves masked by confusion for what we do not comprehend.
She'll love you, but fuck your shit up if you disrespect her.

Do you know God?
Yes, but I'm afraid our interpretations are not one and the same.

Dear God

Why? Is the question of the day, just as it is every other day.

I'm as a jigsaw puzzle piece.

You cut me different and you know that you did.

You left me. No leads to my missing link.

I'm trapped in a box where the scene on the outside doesn't match this piece that is jumping on the inside.

Looking for the rest of my pieces.

They appear to be nothing more than fallen chips that lay dispersed on the floor.

Can there be such a thing as happiness on Earth?

A place where every truth is not a lie and every lie is...well...a lie?

Uncover their eyes because they are not obedient enough to see no evil.

Unplug their ears because they aren't conscious enough to hear no evil.

Unseal their lips because before their thoughts are finished, they have spoken every evil that you can think of. To be cursed is to be loved in this godforsaken place called Earth.

Dear God, you say that this world will never again end in a flood, but what will wash away our sins and the blood of our kin?

Ashes to ashes. Dust to dust.

Flesh of our flesh, and blood of our blood.

Where do I belong?

Dear God, are you listening?

Can there be such a thing as happiness…pure happiness, living on Earth?

Serenity

I found serenity the day that serenity found me

She approached me at the weakest moment of my life. I had to steal her from the CVS aisle of my mind

The moment that I met serenity she gazed into my eyes and kissed me upon my cheek, leaving nothing but the indent line from her lips upon my face

I had not known serenity

She pressed her chest up against the palm of my hand so close that I could feel her words speak to me with her mouth closed

Serenity was soft to touch as her handless body extended the lifeline in the palm of my hand

I was lost

She found me

The day she looked me in the eyes was the beginning of a new life, began again

Rebirth appeared to me

Aisle 5. Her scent captivated me and caught my attention

Aisle 4. She whispered my name, in my mind the demons dispersed into different directions

Aisle 3. I picked her up and asked her to take a walk with me…still so stunned by her ability to steal the attention of *InnerG*

Aisle 2. My feet picked up the pace and I started running so that no one could see

Passing Aisle 1. I noticed people watching but I didn't stop because I didn't want them to take serenity away from me

Checkout. Getting nervous but I still bend corners, hoping that I reach the exit before the sliding doors close

Outside. My heart is racing and I can't breathe in through my nose

But this feeling is what I prayed for and in my darkest moment God sent her to me

He granted me peace

He granted me peace

He gave me…serenity

God is Angry

I saw God speak to me in a dream

She/He was angry

As clouds maneuvered their way around the sky, *she* opened up her mouth and blew them away, allowing rays of sunlight to illuminate *her* bosom

I watched her blow them down until they became small and insignificant, and soon after nonexistent

She blew me toward them

They gently fell at my feet

He created a whirlwind in the sky and sucked in a trail of balloons that had been sent *his* way to admire

Almost in the very same breath, he chewed them up and spit them back out, deflating what was left of the bundle as they gently fell into the fields

I turned to my friend and whispered, "God is angry"

She agreed, and in silence we walked to our destination

I saw God speak to me in a dream

He/She was angry

Then it began to rain

A Piece/Peace of Goodness

Sometimes the morning darkness can be brighter than the rising sun

And when she speaks, she utters words of perfection

"Good morning, beautiful!"

I greet her with the response, "Good morning, and thank you for allowing me to share a piece/peace of your space, in the midst of such anarchy"

I feel blessed to have a sound mind, all of my limbs, an able body, love in my heart, and good people at my side

...it is the recognition of the small things *in* life that make the process *of* life more bearable

Untitled

Peace

Beautiful skies

Frightening stares

Glowing eyes

Sweet dreams everlasting speaking a precious wage

Singing a new song

Humming a new word

Sweet dreams everlasting to you

Made in the USA
San Bernardino, CA
29 July 2019